THE
DIVERSIFIED TABLE

With a Latin Twist

Alina Freyre

THE DIVERSIFIED TABLE
With a Latin Twist

iUniverse books may be ordered through booksellers or by contacting:

iUniverse
1663 Liberty Drive
Bloomington, IN 47403
www.iuniverse.com
1-800-Authors (1-800-288-4677)

Because of the dynamic nature of the Internet, any web addresses or links contained in this book may have changed since publication and may no longer be valid. The views expressed in this work are solely those of the author and do not necessarily reflect the views of the publisher, and the publisher hereby disclaims any responsibility for them.

Any people depicted in stock imagery provided by Thinkstock are models, and such images are being used for illustrative purposes only.
Certain stock imagery © Thinkstock.

ISBN: 978-1-5320-3820-4 (sc)
ISBN: 978-1-5320-3821-1 (e)

Library of Congress Control Number: 2017918861

Print information available on the last page.

iUniverse rev. date: 02/08/2018

DEDICATION

Thank you to the loves of my life;
Andy, Andy Jr and Gaby
for always believing in me and encouraging me,
no matter what my adventure was.
I dedicate this to book to the three of you
and hope you always know that I love you more, most, first!

INTRODUCTION

Cooking has been a passion of mine since I can remember, but my inspiration took a new focus in 2008 when my son was diagnosed with type 1 diabetes. I had just finished a certificate program at a local culinary school, was the owner of a catering company and was about to open a bistro when we got the call from the doctor. Within a few months, things got so overwhelming that I realized cooking for the masses was taking me down a road that I was not enjoying. I closed my bistro and took a break from cooking until 2009, when my family gifted me with a leather-bound journal.

They reminded me of my passion and told me to start writing all my experimental recipes in hope that I could eventually turn it into a cookbook. It was at that moment that I realized cooking needed to be much more intimate than cooking for the masses. During the next eight years, I struggled with a large weight gain and several personal issues. It took me a long time to get to where I am today, and I knew that for me to get to a healthy state in my life, physically and emotionally, I had to make some permanent changes. I decided to change my eating habits extremely and became a pescatarian. This really helped me be conscious of what I was eating. My son had chosen a vegetarian path several months earlier, so I had already been used to cooking simply vegetable dishes. All of us, my husband, my son, my daughter and myself became a tighter unit by choosing to eat healthy together. Now we had a vegetarian, a pescatarian and 2 lean meat eaters and this became the inspiration for the title of the cookbook, "The Diversified Table".

My goal for this cookbook is simple, to share delicious recipes with others. I am no longer afraid to eat, I am just conscious of what and how much. I also hope to help those that are intimidated at times with all the different options and possibilities. As you go through the cookbook, I will share with you my tricks and tips that I have learned through the years and that have allowed me to express myself and grow as a better chef. I will also share stories and memories of why and when I was inspired to create each recipe. The recipes that I have chosen in this book are staples in my home and dinner parties and have similar cooking technique and spices. I will also teach you how to make 2 or 3 separate recipes by changing or adding one or a few ingredients. Coming from a Cuban family I enjoy Latin flavors and you will find that you do not need too many spices or herbs to cook many different meals.

I hope you enjoy all my recipes the way my family and friends have.

Ali

CONTENTS

TRICKS AND TIPS IN THE KITCHEN

- **_Pots and Pans_** – there are so many types of pots and pans not to mention all the sizes they come in. If you can't afford (whether financially or lack of space) I feel it is better to have a few medium and large pots and/or pans. Also note that you do not have to have every pot/pan come with a lid since the lids are usually interchangeable. Below is a quick guide on the different types and the different materials available. I can assure you that you usually do not need every material and I would recommend that you stick to the pot/pan you would use the most often and chances are you can cook almost all your meals in it.
    - Types
        - Saucepans
            - Usually to boil or cook foods in sauce
            - Very versatile for many recipes
        - Sauté Pan or Wok
            - Great for sautéing vegetables
        - Skillet or Cast Iron
            - Good for searing foods
            - Good for browning foods
        - Dutch Oven
            - Great for stove top or oven use
            - Stock Pot
            - Larger pot
            - Good for stocks or soups
    - Materials
        - Aluminum
            - Reactive with acidic foods or alkaline
            - Scratches easily

- Affordable
- Excellent conductor of heat
    - Anodized Aluminum
        - Excellent conductor of heat
        - Scratch-resistant
        - Coated to protect
        - Better alternative to plain aluminum
    - Cast Iron
        - Conducts heat evenly
        - Durable
        - Reactive
        - Heavy
        - Needs maintenance
    - Enameled Cast Iron
        - Non-reactive
        - Easy to clean
        - Excellent alternative to raw cast iron
        - Beautiful and comes in many colors
    - Non-Stick
        - Non-reactive
        - Easy to clean
        - Good for sticky foods
    - Stainless steel
        - Most versatile
        - Non-reactive
        - Dishwasher safe
        - Poor heat distribution

- **_Knives_** – can be intimidating, especially with the number of styles and shapes. I remember in culinary school being the most nervous in my first class that taught knife skills. We had to take a timed final to show our knife skills and I was so scared of cutting myself. Me and blood do not mix well together. Anyway, I got through and now learning how to use a knife properly is probably my most valued skill. You do not need to have all the knives, but you should have at least one good, sharp knife that is very versatile. Below is a list of the knives I feel are the most useful in everyday cooking.

- Chef Knife
  - Most versatile
  - Good for almost everything
- Paring knife
  - Good for more precise cutting
  - Good for peeling and fruits
- Carving knife
  - Good for carving meats
  - Men like this on Thanksgiving (LOL)
- Kitchen Shears
  - Who would think a pair of scissors would be important but when you are afraid of the knife, you can do a lot with the shears
  - Good for cutting herbs
  - Good for breaking bones
  - Good for just opening food packages

- ***Importance of chopping*** – Size does matter in cooking. When you read through the ingredients and it states the size of the dice or the shape of the cut, there is a specific reason for this. Since vegetables cook at different speeds, it is important that their size is uniform, so they will cook evenly. It also important to follow the instructions and cook the vegetables in the right order for the same reason. Something that I like to do at the beginning of the week or after my big trip to the grocery is to cut all the vegetables and place them in bags for quick use. This always ensures that I cook since I know I don't always have to be in the kitchen chopping. If you are unsure what you will be making for the week, dice everything medium since you can always cut them smaller if needed.

This leads to another skill I learned in culinary school and my last trick and probably my most important... "Mise en Place"

- **_"Mise en place_**" means everything in its place. I truly believe this is the secret ingredient to being successful in the kitchen. I always make sure to read the recipe first and then I make sure that I have all the ingredients to successfully cook the dish. I will admit that sometimes I like to challenge myself and change some of the ingredients for others based on what I have in the kitchen or what my taste buds are craving. It is not enough to just have the ingredients, you also need to have the proper utensils/ equipment, the pot(s) and/or pan(s) ready and most important, all the ingredients cleaned, diced and measured. Once you are ready, read through the recipe again and make sure that the cooking time coincides with the time you want to serve your meal. Once you master your mise en place, you will be more relaxed in the kitchen and your food skills will change completely.

- Enjoy cooking and make it a family affair, I promise you will not be sorry!

SPANGLISH DICTIONARY

Café
Coffee
Camarones
Shrimp
Churrasco
Skirt Steak
Croqueta
Croquette
Duquesa
Duchess
Empanada
Patty
Enchilado

Fricase
Fricassee
Fuerte
Strong
Garbanzo
Chick Peas
Gazpacho
Gazpacho
Guayaba
Guava
Leche
Milk

Maduros
Ripe Plantain
Malanga
Malanga
Mariquitas
Green plantain chips
Pastelitos
Pastries
Picadillo
Minced Meat
Plato
Plate
Pollo
Chicken
Queso Crema
Cream Cheese
Sopa
Soup
Tostones
Green Plantain

Appetizers are usually served prior to the start of a meal. I like to think of appetizers as a little more than just a starter. The type of appetizers you will find in this cook book can be served during brunch, lunch or dinner. That's the fun part about cooking, there are no rules.

appetizers

Avocado and Egg Toast
Bacon and Cheddar Croqueta
Bruschetta
Cowboy Caviar
Empanadas
Garbanzo Frito Hummus
Guayaba & Queso Crema Croissants
Stuffed Tostones

aperitivos

Maduro Bread
Malanga Chips
Mariquitas
Pastelitos
Shrimp Ceviche
Stuffed Tostones
Wild Mushroom Crostini

AVOCADO AND EGG TOAST

Serves 4-6

I love this dish and any restaurant that serves this is always a must for me to order. So of course, I would have to have my own recipe. I know that many recipes have many ingredients, but I like mine simple enough that I can taste the avocado and the egg.

- 1 Hass avocado (cut in small cubes)
- 4 hard-boiled eggs
- 2 green onion (chopped small)
- 1 teaspoon lime juice
- 1 tablespoon olive oil

- ¼ teaspoon garlic powder
- ¼ teaspoon Kosher salt
- ⅛ teaspoon pepper
- 2 tablespoon flat leaf parsley (chopped)
- 7 grain toast (8-10 slices)

1. In a bowl mash the eggs with a fork until small pieces
2. Add the avocado and lime juice and mix together until it becomes a little creamy
3. Add the onion, olive oil, garlic powder, salt, pepper and parsley and mix well
4. Serve with toast (I like to cut the toasts into triangles)
5. Place the onion and other ½ of the avocado in a bowl

BACON AND CHEDDAR CROQUETA

Makes about 20

Here in Miami, it is very common to go to a Cuban bakery or restaurant and order a croqueta to start or just for a quick bite. You will usually find ham, chicken or cheese croqueta, so I decided to learn how to make one a little different. The great thing about this recipe is once you learn how to make the base, you can get creative.

- ½ cup all-purpose flour
- 1 ½ cup milk
- ½ cup Vidalia onion (small dice)
- 2 tablespoons olive oil
- 4 tablespoons butter (unsalted)
- 2 eggs

- ½ teaspoon kosher salt
- ¼ teaspoon pepper
- Bread crumbs
- ½ cup cooked bacon
- ½ cup shredded cheddar cheese
- Vegetable oil for frying

1. Grease a 9-inch square pan
2. In a medium sauce pan on medium heat add the olive oil and onion and cook until translucent (4-5 minutes)
3. Add the butter and when melted, add the flour and mix well with a whisk and continue to cook for another 2 minutes
4. Raise the heat to medium high, add ½ the milk and bring to a boil
5. Add remainder of the milk and continue to cook while whisking for another 5 minutes or until mixture thickens
6. Lower the heat to medium and continue to whisk to make sure there is a smooth consistency (about 10 more minutes)
7. Add the bacon, salt and pepper and stir to incorporate well and remove from heat
8. Let cool for about 5 minutes then add the cheese and stir well
9. Spread the mixture evenly in the prepared pan cover and refrigerate overnight
10. Remove from the mass from the fridge, scramble the eggs and add the breading to a shallow dish

11. With a spoon, scoop some of the croquet mass and shape in a circle or oval in about a 1 ½ inch diameter
12. Dip the croqueta in the breading, then the egg, then the breading again and place on a separate platter
13. When all the mass has been molded, place back in the refrigerator for about 30 – 45 minutes
14. Heat the vegetable oil on medium high heat and fry croquetas about 4 at a time
15. When golden brown remove from the oil and place on plate lined with paper towel to drain the excess oil
16. Serve with lime wedges

BRUSCHETTA

Serves a party of 10

I always like to have items in the refrigerator that you can eat with anything. My husband and son love to have something quick to eat when they are hungry or a little something they can add to dishes for a different flavor. This is that recipe, and it is better the next day!

- 3 firm tomatoes (medium dice)
- 1 cubanelle pepper (small dice)
- 1 jalapeno (very small dice – no seeds)
- 1 baby Vidalia onion (white and green part, small dice) — you can substitute with ½ cup Vidalia onion (small dice)
- 3 cloves garlic (minced)
- 1 cup chopped cilantro
- 1 teaspoon cumin
- 1 teaspoon kosher salt
- ½ teaspoon pepper
- ½ cup olive oil (maybe a little more)
- ¼ tablespoon lemon juice
- Cuban bread, sliced and toasted

1. Place the vegetables in a large bowl and mix well
2. Add the salt, pepper, cumin, lemon juice and olive oil; mix well
3. Add the cilantro at the end and mix again
4. Serve with the Cuban bread toast points

BRUSCHETTA IN CUBAN BREAD CROSTINI'S

COWBOY CAVIAR

Serves 4-6

An ex-coworker of mine made this once and I was very amused by the clever name. I happen to love caviar, but this is nothing like what you normally think caviar to be. There are a lot of recipes out there for this, but this one that I have made my own and I think that more people should make this, it is delicious and easy.

- 1 red onion (small dice)
- 1 green pepper (small dice)
- 1 red pepper (small dice)
- 15 ounce can of whole kernel corn (drained and rinsed)
- 15 ounce can of black beans (drained and rinsed)
- 15 ounce can of black eye peas (drained and rinsed)
- 1 cup of cilantro (chopped)
- 3 small tomatoes (medium dice)
- 1 jalapeno (small dice)
- ½ cup olive oil
- ⅓ cup red wine vinegar
- 1 ½ teaspoon kosher salt
- ¾ teaspoon pepper
- ¼ cup sugar

1. Mix everything together well and refrigerate for about an hour. Serve with crackers, zucchini or cucumber chips.

EMPANADAS

Serves 6-8

Empanadas are almost like pastelitos except with a thicker dough and you can either bake them or fry them. In this recipe, we are going to bake them. Since the dough is a little thicker there are more options for fillers.

- Empanada dough discs (I use Goya and you can find them in the frozen food section)
- Variety of left over recipes and/or ingredients

1. Heat the oven to 375 degrees
2. In the of the empanada dough add 2 tablespoons of filling in the middle of the disk
3. Dip your finger in water and wet around the edge of the dough
4. Fold the disk in half to make half a moon shape
5. Take a fork and press around the edges of the dough to seal it
6. Place on a baking sheet lined with parchment paper and bake for about 15 minutes
7. Filler Options
   a. Baked chicken salad – recipe on page 27
   b. Fricassee de pollo – recipe on page 73
   c. Picadillo – recipe on page 80

GARBANZO FRITO HUMMUS

Serves 4-6

This recipe was a spin off from the garbanzos frito recipe. I love hummus and one day when I was making garbanzo's frito, my husband suggested that I turn the entire dish into a hummus and violate.

- 1 Vidalia onion
- 6 cloves of garlic
- 2 cans of garbanzo beans (drained & rinsed)
- 12 ounce can roasted red peppers (medium dice)
- ½ cup tahini paste (optional)
- 8 ounces tomato sauce
- 3 tablespoon olive oil
- 1 teaspoon cumin

- 1 teaspoon smoked paprika
- 1 teaspoon turmeric
- I teaspoon onion powder
- 1 teaspoon garlic powder
- 1 teaspoon dry oregano
- 3 tablespoon fresh flat leaf parsley rough chop
- 2 teaspoon salt
- 1 teaspoon pepper

1. Wrap the red pepper in foil with a little olive oil into a 400° oven and cook for about 20 minutes.
2. In a large sauté pan on medium high heat add the olive oil and cook the onions until translucent (about 5 minutes). Add the garlic and cook for another 1-2 minutes and reduce heat to medium.
3. Add the garbanzos and the red peppers and mix everything well. Add the tomato sauce and all the spices (cumin, smoked paprika, garlic, onion, oregano, salt and pepper) and reduce the heat to low and simmer uncovered for about 15 -20 minutes.
4. Remove from heat and let cool for about 30 minutes.
5. In a large muddle, add the garbanzos, add the parsley and muddle until consistency desired (I like to leave some garbanzos with some larger pieces).
6. You can also add them to a food processor along with the parsley and tahini paste, and puree to give it more of the typical hummus appearance.

GARBANZO FRITO HUMMUS

GUAYABA Y QUESO CREMA CROISSANT

Serves 4-6

Croissants are a great thing to have handy. They are good for so many recipes or simply to have warm with a cup of coffee. Today was the day after Hurricane Irma hit Florida and since I cooked almost everything I had in the fridge, there was not much. However, my son brought a lot of cream cheese from his store and I had to do something with them. I had croissant dough and guava shells, and this is what we made, delicious!

- 8-ounce tube of Pillsbury Grands Crescent
- 4 guava shells in syrup (diced small)
- ½ cup cream cheese
- non-stick spray

1. Heat the oven to 350 degrees (based on what the package states)
2. Mix the guava and cream cheese together in a bowl until well incorporated
3. With the non-stick spray a baking sheet
4. Roll out the dough in a flat sheet
5. Place about a tablespoon on the larger portion of the dough and spread so most of the dough is covered. If it needs more, add more.
6. Roll up the dough to form the croissant shape and pinch the edges so the mix does not spill out
7. Place on the baking sheet and cook in the oven for 15 minutes and serve

GUAYAVA & QUESO CREMA CROISSANT

MADURO BREAD

Serves 8-10

We love bananas in our home and we love cake, so I got in the habit of making banana bread. I added the Maduros for a little kick, but you can make this same recipe without. But it is worth the extra work to add them.

- 3 ripe bananas (mashed)
- ⅓ cup butter (5 tablespoons melted)
- 1 teaspoon of baking soda
- ⅛ teaspoon salt
- 1 cup sugar

- 1 large egg (beaten)
- 1 teaspoon pure vanilla extract
- 1 ½ cup flour
- 1 ripe plantain "Maduro" (sliced)
- 2 teaspoons cinnamon (optional)

1. Fry the plantains first in a little vegetable oil and place on a paper toweled plate to dry and cool; once cool cut into small pieces
2. Preheat the oven to 350 degrees and butter a loaf pan (9 x 5)
3. In a bowl, with a fork, mash the bananas well until almost liquid
4. Add to the banana mix, butter, sugar, salt, vanilla and baking soda, mixing well between each ingredient with a large spoon
5. Add flour in three parts and mix well each time
6. Fold the maduros into the batter
7. Sprinkle the cinnamon on the top (if you like cinnamon you can add a little more)
8. Bake in the oven for about 50 – 55 minutes until a toothpick is inserted and comes out clean

BANANA "MADURO" BREAD

MALANGA CHIPS
with cilantro garlic aioli
Serves 4-6

When I was younger we used to go to a restaurant called Isla Canaria they used to have these in addition to mariquitas. These are more like potato chips then the mariquitas but when they are homemade, the edges are crunchy and the middle a little softer and they are so delicious.

- 4 Malanga's peeled and sliced very thin
- Kosher salt to season
- 2 cups vegetable oil

Aioli
- ¾ cup avocado oil mayo (or regular mayo)
- 3 cloves garlic (minced)
- 1 tablespoon lime juice
- 2 tablespoon cilantro

1. In a medium sauce pot on medium to medium high heat add the oil
2. Add the Malanga in batches until golden brown
3. Remove from heat with a slotted spoon and drain on a plate layered with a towel
4. Sprinkle with the salt as you remove fried batches
5. For the aioli, add the garlic and a pinch of salt in a food processor and pulse
6. Add the mayo, cilantro and lime juice and blend well

MARIQUITAS
con mojo
Serves 4-6

Mariquitas are fried bananas that are not sweet but salty and when you dip them in mojo (a garlic sauce) the flavor is out of this world. Most people eat them like chips or as an appetizer and they are usually served on a plate as a large mountain before the meal. They are so simple to make and very worth it.

- 3 green plantains (sliced very thin)
- 1 cup of mojo (recipe on pag 72)
- Kosher salt to season
- 2 cups vegetable oil

1. In a medium sauce pot on medium to medium high heat add the oil
2. Add the plantain in batches until golden brown
3. Remove from heat with a slotted spoon and drain on a plate layered with a towel
4. Sprinkle with the salt as you remove fried batches
5. Add the mojo to a blender and liquefy
6. Dip the mariquita in the mojo or pour over

MARIQUITAS

PASTELITOS

Serves 4-6

You can go to any Cuban restaurant and find pastelitos and usually you can only find a few types. However, if you learn how to make them you can add many fillings and create all kinds. This is another recipe that you can make by reusing many recipes that I have already added to this cook book.

- Puff pastry dough sheets (you can find this in many groceries)
- Egg wash (1 egg and 3 teaspoons of water mixed together)
- Simple syrup (¼ cup sugar and ¼ cup water heated until sugar is dissolved and then cooled)
- Variety of left over recipes and/or ingredients

1. Preheat the oven to 375 degrees
2. Cut the dough in the shape you want with a cookie cutter (about 4 inches in diameter)
3. You can cut them in different shapes based on what flavor you want to use
4. Make sure to have a bottom and a top layer
5. Add the filler in the middle of the dough, make sure to leave 1-inch diameter around
6. Dip your finger in water and wet around the bottom edge of the dough
7. Place the top portion of the dough on top of the filler and press around the edge of the dough to seal them together
8. Place on a baking sheet lined with parchment paper
9. Brush the top of the pastries with a little of the egg wash
10. Place in the oven and cook for about 20 minutes (golden brown)
11. Brush a little of the simple syrup on top of each pastelito
12. Filler options
    a. Picadillo (cold) – recipe on page 80
    b. Guava paste and cream cheese
        i. 1 ½ inch long guava paste
        ii. 1 inch long cream cheese
    c. *Fricassee de pollo (cold) – recipe on page 73*

PASTELITOS DE CARNE, GUAVA AND CREAM CHEESE AND EMPANADAS

SHRIMP CEVICHE

Serves 4-6

Ceviche is such a great dish to make ahead, since the shrimp has to cook in the citrus. Since I became a pescatarian, I make this dish all the time. You can serve it with cucumber chips or crackers.

- 1 pound high- quality raw medium size shrimp (peeled, deveined and sliced in half)
- 1 small red onion (small dice)
- 1 yellow pepper (small dice)
- 1 jalapeno (very small dice)
- ½ cup chopped cilantro

- ⅔ cup freshly squeezed lemon juice
- ⅓ cup freshly squeezed lime juice
- 2 tablespoon orange juice
- 1 teaspoon kosher salt
- ½ teaspoon white pepper
- ⅓ cup mango (small dice)

1. In a large bowl (3 quarts) add the shrimp, onion, jalapeno, yellow pepper, lemon, lime and orange juice, salt, pepper and mango and mix well
2. Place in the refrigerator for about 1 hour
3. Add the cilantro, mix and serve

SHRIMP CEVICHE

STUFFED TOSTONES

Serves 4-6

Another common appetizer you find in a Cuban restaurant but it such a great dish since you can use the tostones as a vessel and stuff it with anything you want. In this dish, I will teach you how to make the tostones and then give you some recommendations of dishes that I have throughout this cookbook use as the stuffing. You will need a plantain press for this (if you don't have one, you can mold them with a small coffee cup)

- 2 green plantain bananas (peeled and cut about 1 ½ inches thick)
- Vegetable oil (for frying)

1. Place the oil in a medium size Dutch oven or saucepan on medium to medium high heat
2. Fry the plantains until light brown
3. Remove from the oil and place on a plate with paper towel to dry off the oil
4. Place the plantain in the press and shape into a cup
5. Place the shape plantain back in the oil and cook until more golden brown
6. Place back on paper towel and sprinkle with salt before it cools off
   a. Serving options
   b. Picadillo – recipe on page 80
   c. Fricassee de pollo recipe on page 73
   d. Camarones enchilada recipe on page 67

WILD MUSHROOM CROSTINI

Serves 4-6

I make this all the time and is a staple to my appetizer repertoire. It is so simple to make and yet looks like you slaved over the dish. Did I mention it is delicious? If you can't find all the different mushrooms or you only like a certain type, feel free to change them.

- 3 shallots (cut in half and small dice)
- 2 cups baby bella mushrooms (small dice)
- 1 cup shitake mushrooms (small dice)
- 1 cup oyster mushrooms (small dice)
- 2 cups cremini mushrooms (small dice)
- 1 tablespoon olive oil
- 4 ounces goat cheese
- 1 teaspoon sea salt
- ½ teaspoon pepper
- French baguette (sliced ½ inch thick)

1. Preheat the oven to 350 degrees
2. Place the slices of baguette to a baking sheet and bake about 5 minutes until crisp (optional)
3. On a large non-stick sauté pan on medium heat add the oil
4. Add the shallots and the mushrooms and cook until tender
5. Add the salt and pepper and mix well
6. To serve, spread some goat cheese on a slice of baguette and top with mushroom mix

WILD MUSHROOM CROSTINI WITH GOAT CHEESE

Salads are a great way to have a fulfilling meal with many different flavors and textures that will fill you up. Same can be said about soups. I will usually start with a small salad or cup of soup before my meal for 2 reasons, 1 – to taste something extra and 2 – so I won't eat too much during dinner.

salad

Baked Chicken Salad
Arugala Salad
Neptune Salad

ensalada

Strawberry Fields Salad
Tuna Pasta Salad

soup

Cuban Chili
Garlic Soup
Gazpacho

sopa

Malanga Puree
Sopa de Pollo

ARUGALA SALAD
with apples and gorgonzola
Serves 4 – 6

Arugula has such a delicious and distinct flavor by itself, but when you pair it with different layers, it simply enhances it to another level. I love apples with cheese so why not make a salad with all these ingredients combined.

- 1 Granny Smith apple, (medium dice)
- 3 cups Arugula (washed and dried)
- ¼ cup red onion (small dice)
- 5 tablespoons Gorgonzola, crumbled
- 5 tablespoons glazed pecans
- 2 tablespoons olive oil and vinegar dressing

Dressing
- ¼ cup white wine vinegar
- ½ cup extra-virgin olive oil
- 2 tablespoons Dijon mustard
- ½ teaspoon kosher salt
- ¼ teaspoon black pepper

1. In a small bowl add the olive oil, vinegar, Dijon mustard, salt and pepper and whisk well
2. In a separate larger bowl, add the arugula, apples, onions, gorgonzola and pecans
3. Pour dressing over the salad; start with half and then toss
4. Continue to add dressing if needed

BAKED CHICKEN SALAD

Serves 4-6

Chicken salad is one of those classic dishes that is easy to make and has the potential of mixing salt and sweet flavors together. You can also make a multitude of different recipes.

- Cooked whole chicken chopped and deboned
- ½ cup granny smith apple (small dice)
- ¼ cup red onion (small dice)
- ½ teaspoon kosher salt
- ¼ teaspoon pepper
- ½ cup celery (small dice)
- ½ cup cucumber (medium dice)
- ¼ cup yellow raisins
- ½ tablespoon lemon juice
- 2 tablespoon avocado oil mayo (or any mayo you like will do)

1. Add all the ingredients in a large bowl and mix well
2. Serve as a sandwich on toasted bread or over a bed of lettuce

BAKED CHICKEN SALAD

NEPTUNE SALAD

Serves 4-6

You know how you always go to the grocery store and there is some sort of seafood salad premade by the fish department? Well I always look at them and want to buy them, but I get nervous that there may be relish in it, which I do not like, but since it looks so tasty I decided to make my own version

- 12 ounces of imitation crab meat
- 12 ounces of medium shrimp (cleaned, deveined and cooked)
- 7 ounce can of white Albacore tuna (in water, drained)
- ½ teaspoon Kosher salt
- ¼ teaspoon pepper
- ½ cup red onion (small dice)
- ½ cup cucumber (small dice)
- 1 garlic clove (minced)
- ¼ cup celery (small dice)
- ½ cup avocado oil mayo (or any mayo)
- ½ tablespoon lemon juice
- 1 teaspoon fresh flat leaf parsley (chopped)

1. Chop the crab and shrimp to desired sizes, I like them medium size chop then add to a medium size bowl along with the tuna
2. Add the rest of the ingredients to the crab, shrimp and tuna mix and stir well
3. Serve chilled

NEPTUNE SALAD

STRAWBERRY FIELDS SALAD

Serves 2-4

Whenever I crave a salad, I usually crave a light, refreshing one and enjoy fruits and nuts as a part of it. I went through a huge craving pattern when I was pregnant with my daughter for a specific salad that had raspberries and goat cheese. Recently I found a goat cheese that was made with homey and I thought I would take my original salad recipe flavors and create a new one.

- 6 cups mixed greens and red leaf lettuce (rinsed and dried)
- 1 cup strawberries (sliced)
- ½ cup grape tomatoes (sliced in half)
- 4 tablespoons honey goat cheese
- 1 cup pecans
- 2 green onions (chopped)
- 20 – 24 Shrimp (peeled, cleaned and deveined - optional)

- 2 tablespoon olive oil

Agave Mustard Dressing
- ¼ cup Dijon mustard
- ¼ cup Agave syrup
- ¼ cup apple cider vinegar
- 1 teaspoon salt
- ½ cup walnut oil

1. In a small bowl, mix the mustard, Agave, vinegar, salt and oil and whisk well until blended
2. In a separate large bowl add the lettuce, strawberries, green onions and pecans. Drizzle about 1-2 tablespoons of the dressing and toss the salad well so that all the lettuce is coated
3. In a medium non-stick sauté pan on medium-high heat, add olive oil and sauté the shrimp until pink and browned, about 3-5 minutes
4. Add the goat cheese and mix one last time.

STRAWBERRY FIELDS SALAD

TUNA PASTA SALAD

Serves 6-8

I remember the start of this recipe when I was in high school with a friend of mine that would make one similar. It was always one of my favorites and since I love to make recipes that I are just as good if not better after they sit in the fridge overnight, makes this recipe one of my favorites. I have even been able to get young kids to like this one.

- 1-pound box of tri-color rotini pasta
- 12 ounce can of Albacore Tuna (in water)
- ⅓ cup red pepper (small dice)
- ⅓ cup green pepper (small dice)
- ⅓ cup yellow pepper (small dice)
- ½ cup Vidalia onion (small dice)
- ⅓ cup celery (small dice)
- 1 cup grape tomatoes (sliced thin)
- ⅓ cup Kalamata olives (sliced thin)
- 2 tablespoons avocado mayo
- 2 tablespoons low fat cream cheese (I prefer whipped)
- 2 teaspoons Kosher salt (1 for the pasta water and one for the salad)
- ½ teaspoon pepper
- ½ teaspoon garlic powder
- 1 tablespoon fresh parsley (rough chop)
- 1 cup zesty Italian dressing (I prefer Wishbone or Kraft)

1. In a large sauce pan boil the pasta and 1 teaspoon of the salt until al dente (about 8-10 minutes)
2. Drain the pasta and let cool for about 20-30 minutes
3. Drain the tuna well and place in a large mixing bowl
4. Add the onion, red, green and yellow peppers, tomatoes, celery, olives, mayo, cream cheese, remaining salt, pepper and garlic powder and mix well then place in the fridge until the pasta is cooled
5. Pour the dressing and parsley all over the pasta and mix well to make sure the pasta is well coated
6. Mix in the tuna well and serve or continue to chill

CUBAN CHILI

Serves 6-8

Chili is one of those recipes that warms the soul and is good to eat at practically any time in day. Since I hate wasted food I developed this recipe from two recipes in this cookbook with a few additions

- Picadillo (recipe page 80)
- Ali's black beans (recipe page 44)
- 12 ounces of crushed tomatoes
- 1 tablespoon lemon juice
- 1 Hass avocado
- 1 cup shredded gouda cheese
- 1 green plantain (shredded like cheese)
- 2 cups vegetable oil
- Cilantro aioli (recipe page 15)

1. In a small sauce pan on medium high heat add the vegetable oil and fry the green plantain in batches then set aside on a plate lined with paper towel to drain excess oil and sprinkle some salt while still hot
2. Make the full picadillo recipe and Ali's black beans and mix together in a large sauce pot on medium heat
3. Add the can of crushed tomatoes and lemon juice to the pot and mix well
4. Serve in a bowl with gouda cheese, avocado, cilantro sour cream and top with grated tostones
5. Grade a green plantain and then flash fry in medium high heat oil until golden brown
6. Remove from the heat with meshed spoon

GARLIC SOUP

Serves 4

My husband and I used to go to this restaurant near our old home where they served Spanish cuisine. One of my favorite dishes was the garlic soup and most of all was the poached egg that was served in the middle. The flavor of this soup was divine and when the restaurant was sold, the food was never the same. I decided that I had to make my own.

- 2 tablespoons olive oil
- 6 slices of bread (crusts removed, cut into ½ inch cubes)
- 6 garlic cloves (minced)
- 2 green onions, green part only (chopped)
- ¾ teaspoon smoked paprika
- 1 teaspoon Salt
- 5 ½ cups chicken stock
- 4 poached eggs

1. In a large sauce pot on medium high heat add the oil and the bread
2. Cook for about 4-5 minutes until toasted and lightly browned
3. Add the garlic, green onion, salt and smoked paprika and stir well, cook for another 2 minutes
4. Pour the stock into the pot and bring to a boil. Reduce the heat and simmer for 15 minutes
5. Before you serve, add each egg to a small ramekin and slowly drop into the soup, one at a time
6. Try to keep them separate to serve one per person
7. Cook eggs about 3-4 minutes then serve immediately
8. Ladle some soup into a bowl and top with a poached egg

GAZPACHO

Serves 4-6

I made this recipe a lot when I had my catering company. Not only was it easy to make, it was delicious. This recipe is great for the hot summer days in Miami. I like to serve it in a champagne glass to make it look elegant.

- 4 large tomatoes – medium dice
- 1 cup cucumber (peeled) – medium dice
- ½ cup green pepper - medium dice
- ½ cup red pepper - medium dice
- 1 cup Vidalia onion – medium dice
- 3 cloves garlic
- 2 cups grape tomatoes

- 1 ½ teaspoon salt
- 1 teaspoon pepper
- 2 tablespoon lime juice
- ¼ cup olive oil
- 1 tablespoon Italian parsley – chopped
- 1 tablespoon cilantro - chopped

1. Set oven to 450 degrees
2. In tin foil, add the garlic, red pepper, green pepper and onion with 1 teaspoon of olive oil and roast for about 20 – 25 minutes then let cool
3. In a blender, add to tomatoes, cucumber, green and red peppers, onion, garlic, salt, pepper, lime juice, olive oil, parsley and cilantro and blend well
4. If you want a fine consistency, pour through a strainer
5. Serve with a drizzle of olive oil

GAZPACHO

MALANGA PUREE
with cilantro cream
Serves 4

I am not a huge fan of mashed potatoes, but I do enjoy puree de malanga and it is very good for you. This is a hearty style soup and could be a meal replacement if you serve yourself enough. You can also serve it as a side dish in place of the typical mashed potatoes.

- 2 pounds Malanga
- 1 Vidalia onion (small dice)
- 10 garlic cloves (minced)
- 1 tablespoon olive oil
- 6 cups vegetable stock
- ½ cup heavy cream
- ½ teaspoon Kosher salt

- ¼ teaspoon pepper
- ½ teaspoon garlic powder

Cilantro Cream
- 8 ounces sour cream
- ¼ cup cilantro
- ¼ teaspoon Kosher salt
- 1/8 teaspoon white pepper
- ¼ teaspoon lime juice

1. Peel, wash and cut the Malanga into small pieces
2. Place in a large Dutch oven with enough water to cover the Malanga and boil for 20 minutes
3. Drain the water and place the Malanga on a plate
4. In the same Dutch oven on medium heat add the olive oil and sauté the onion until translucent, about 4-5 minutes
5. Add the garlic and cook for another 2 minutes and then add the Malanga and the broth, bring to a boil and then lower the heat and simmer until the Malanga is tender, about 30- 40 minutes
6. Remove from the heat and blend with an emulsion blender or in a blender until creamy
7. Put back on the heat on low and add the cream, salt, pepper and garlic powder and stir well
8. Mix all ingredients for cilantro cream and serve on top

MALANGA SOUP (PUREE DE MALANGA) WITH CILANTRO CREAM

SOPA DE POLLO

Serves 4-6

I don't know anyone who hasn't had a bowl of Chicken Soup at one time in their life. It's hardy, delicious and good for the soul. My daughter loves to chicken soup with Cuban bread. It's her go to whenever and I almost feel like everyone should have at least one chicken soup recipe.

- 8 cups of chicken stock or veggie stock
- 6 chicken thighs (bone in and skinless)
- 1 cup baby carrots (cups in half)
- 1 cup celery (chopped)
- 2 cups Vidalia onion (large dice)
- 1 cup baby red potatoes (large dice, skin on)
- 2 corns (cut into 1-inch rounds)
- 6 garlic cloves (minced)
- 3 cloves garlic (minced)
- 1 teaspoon smoked paprika
- 1 teaspoon turmeric
- 1 teaspoon ground ginger
- 2 teaspoon Salt
- 1 teaspoon pepper
- 1 tablespoon olive oil
- ¼ cup cilantro (chopped)
- 1 lime (sliced)

1. In a large sauce pot on medium high heat add the oil, onion, carrots and celery
2. Cook for about 3-4 minutes until onion is translucent
3. Add the garlic and cook for about 1-2 minutes
4. Add the chicken thighs and let brown on each side, about 3-4 minutes each side
5. Add the potatoes, paprika, ginger, turmeric, salt and pepper stir well
6. Add the stock and bring to a boil
7. Lower heat and simmer covered for 1 hour
8. Add the cilantro and serve with a slice of lime

SOPA DE POLLO

Side dishes at times go under rated but if you take your time and select the right pairing you can make a simple meal into an extravagant meal. Also know that side dishes can stand alone.

side dish

Ali's Black Beans
Butternut Squash Hash
Garbanzo's Espanola
Greek Peas
Italian Spinach Sauté
Mashed Garlic Yucca
Mediterranean Garbanzos

plato de acompanamento

Rice
    Coconut Rice
    Garlic Rice
    Mushroom Garlic Rice
Roasted Garlic Sprouts
Spicy Green Beans
Zucchini Parmesan Pancakes

ALI'S BLACK BEANS
Serves 4-6

My husband loves his rice and beans, so of course I had to have a recipe that would knock his socks off and after many trials, this is it. Not only is this recipe good as a side dish with rice or alone, it is better the next day, it can be turned into a soup or a sauce by pureeing it.

- 1 red pepper (small dice)
- 1 green pepper (small dice)
- 1 Vidalia onion (small dice)
- 3 cloves garlic (minced)
- 3 tablespoon olive oil
- 1 teaspoon red wine vinegar
- ¼ teaspoon cumin
- ½ teaspoon Kosher Salt

- ¼ teaspoon pepper
- ¼ teaspoon turmeric
- ¼ teaspoon smoked paprika
- ¼ teaspoon onion powder
- ¼ teaspoon garlic powder
- 2 bay leaves
- 2 cans black beans (El Ebor is my favorite) – don't drain
- 1 ½ tablespoon fresh chopped cilantro

1. In a medium sauce pan, on medium heat, add the oil, onion and red and green peppers and cook until the onion is translucent (about 5-6 minutes)
2. Add the garlic and cook for a few more minutes (about 1-2 minutes)
3. Add the black beans and stir well mix all the ingredients
4. Add the cumin, salt, pepper, turmeric, smoked paprika, onion powder and garlic powder and mix everything well
5. Add the bay leaves, cover the pan and lower the heat to simmer
6. Simmer for at least 30 minutes
7. Add the red wine vinegar and cilantro and stir well
8. Keep covered until ready to eat and remove bay leaves before serving

ALI'S BLACK BEANS

ALI'S BLACK BEANS OVER GARLIC RICE

BUTTERNUT SQUASH HASH

Serves 4 – 6

My husband decided that he was going to be on strictly no carbs for about 2 weeks and I thought I would try also. I always like to buy certain foods that will act as the main attraction and the try to figure out what I am going to make based on what I am in the mood to eat that day. This day I was hungry and since I had butternut squash and was not eating potatoes, this is what I came up with.

- 4 cups of butternut squash (medium dice)
- 2 cups zucchini (medium dice)
- 1 Vidalia onion (medium dice)
- 3 cloves garlic (minced)
- 8 baby bella mushrooms (medium dice)
- ½ cup tomato (small dice)
- 2 tablespoons cilantro (chopped)
- 3 tablespoon olive oil
- ½ teaspoon garlic powder
- ½ teaspoon smoked paprika
- ½ teaspoon chipotle
- ½ teaspoon turmeric
- ½ teaspoon salt
- ¼ teaspoon pepper
- 8-10 eggs
- Non-stick spray

1. Preheat oven to 400 degrees.
2. In a baking sheet, lay out the butternut squash with 1 tablespoon olive oil and some salt and pepper and roast for about 3 minutes.
3. In a large sauté pan on medium high heat add the rest of the oil and add the onion and zucchini and cook for about 5-6 minutes until onion is translucent.
4. Add the garlic and sauté for another minute then add garlic powder, smoked paprika, turmeric, chipotle, salt and pepper and continue to cook on medium heat.

GARBANZO ESPANOLA

Serves 4-6

This is a very Spanish dish and a great way to eat chickpeas other than the typical way in hummus. My husband and I always order this dish as an appetizer if it's on the menu and it's great to make since most people have caned chickpeas in the pantry. Below this recipe, I simply make the same dish, but add Tahini paste and puree in the food processor and then you have hummus. This was curtesy of my husband who loves to get as creative in the kitchen as me...well almost as creative.

- 1 Vidalia Onion
- 6 cloves of garlic
- 2 cans of garbanzo beans (drained & rinsed)
- 12 ounce can roasted red peppers (medium dice)
- 8 ounces tomato sauce
- 3 tablespoon olive oil
- 1 teaspoon cumin
- 1 teaspoon smoked paprika
- 1 teaspoon turmeric
- 1 teaspoon onion powder
- 1 teaspoon garlic powder
- 1 teaspoon dry oregano
- 3 tablespoons of fresh flat leaf parsley (rough chop)
- 2 teaspoon salt
- 1 teaspoon pepper

1. In a large sauté pan on medium high heat add the olive oil and cook the onions until translucent (about 5 minutes)
2. Add the garlic and cook for another 1-2 minutes and reduce heat to medium
3. Add the garbanzos and the red peppers and mix everything well
4. Add the tomato sauce and all the spices (cumin, smoked paprika, garlic, onion, oregano, salt and pepper) and reduce the heat to low and simmer uncovered for about 15 -20 minutes
5. Add the parsley at the end, stir well and serve

GARBANZO ESPANOLA

GREEK STYLE PEAS

Serves 6-8

I cannot tell a lie, peas have never been on my must have list, in fact they were on my do not have list...until a friend ours made me taste them cooked like this. Through the years, I have added my touch to the recipe and now I am proud to say that peas are definitely on my "must" have list.

- 16 ounce frozen bag of peas (thawed and drained)
- 8 ounce can tomato sauce
- 1 tablespoon tomato paste
- 2 teaspoon dried oregano
- 1 teaspoon dry dill
- 2 teaspoon kosher salt
- 1 teaspoon pepper
- 2 teaspoon cumin
- 2 teaspoon turmeric
- 1 Vidalia onion (small dice)
- 5 gloves garlic (minced)
- 3 bay leaves
- 3 teaspoon olive oil
- Feta cheese (crumbled)

1. In a 10" (3 quarts) sauté pan on medium to medium high heat add the olive oil and onions and cook until translucent (about 5-6 minutes)
2. Add the garlic and cook for about 1-2 more minutes
3. Add the peas, tomato sauce and the tomato paste along with the oregano, dill, salt, pepper, cumin and turmeric and mix everything well
4. Add the bay leaves, cover and lower the heat to simmer (about 45 minutes)
5. Serve with feta cheese and remove bay leaves before serving

ITALIAN SPINACH SAUTÉ

Serves 4-6

This is one of my most recent recipes that I have created. I am very much into creating very tasty, simple and healthy sides since I started eating 5 times a day. This is a great side that goes with many of the fish recipes in this cook book or just as a snack.

- 1 ½ pounds (3- 9ounce bags) spinach
- ½ cup tomato (small dice)
- 8 cloves garlic (minced)
- 2 tablespoons olive oil
- ¼ cup parmesan cheese (grated)
- 2 teaspoon salt
- 2 teaspoon dry oregano
- 1 teaspoon pepper

1. Rinse the spinach and dry (I love to use a salad spinner).
2. In a large sauté pan on medium heat, add the oil and the spinach and cook for 30 seconds.
3. Add the garlic and cook for an additional minute and then add the tomato and spices. Cook for another 1-2 minutes and then remove from the heat. Add the parmesan cheese and serve.

MASHED YUCCA
con mojo
Serves 6

This is my version of Latin mashed potatoes with a twist. This common Cuban dish for Christmas slightly changed to appeal my pallet and hopefully yours.

- 2 pounds of yucca (peeled and cut into 1-inch pieces)
- 1 tablespoon lime juice
- 1 teaspoon Kosher salt

- 3-4 cups Mojo (recipe on page 72)
- Non-stick spray

1. In a medium stock pot on medium high heat add the yucca and add water to the cover the yucca
2. Add the lime juice and the salt and boil for about About 90 minutes (or until yucca is tender)
3. Drain, add back to pot but remove from heat and add the yucca
4. Mix in the mojo and stir well (use as much mojo as you want)
5. If not serving immediately warm in the pot

MEDITERRANEAN GARBANZOS

Serves 4-6

Chickpeas are so versatile and can be made with so many different flavors. They are also tasty hot or cold and can be made in advance. The other day I was experimenting for lunch and I had a can of garbanzos and had many Greek flavors in the fridge. On the first try it was so delicious it made it straight to the book.

- 2 - 16-ounce cans garbanzos (drained and rinsed)
- 1 cup red onion (sliced thin)
- 2 cloves garlic (minced)
- 2 tablespoon olive oil
- ½ cup feta cheese
- 2 teaspoon dry oregano
- 2 teaspoon salt
- 1 teaspoon pepper
- 1 tablespoon lemon juice

1. In a medium sauté pan on medium heat add the oil, onion and garlic and cook for about 2 minutes. Add the garbanzos and cook for another 2-3 minutes.
2. Add the salt, pepper, oregano and lemon juice and stir well.
3. Continue to cook for another 2 minutes and then remove from the heat. Add the feta cheese, stir and serve.

RICES

COCONUT RICE
Serves 4-6

Well, to say that I love coconut is an understatement. But when I went to this restaurant with my husband, I was blown away with their coconut rice. Needless to say, I had to recreate it at home so that I could have it whenever I wanted. I am very happy with the recipe, but I think I have to go to the restaurant again to make sure. Shout out to Hob Nob in Naples, FL!

- 2 cups Valencia rice
- 1 cup water
- 2 cups coconut milk
- 1 teaspoon salt

1. In a medium sauce pan add the rice, water, milk and salt and bring to a boil. Reduce to medium heat, cover and cook for about 15 minutes
2. With a fork, fluff the rice and lower the heat to low, cover and let sit until ready to serve

GARLIC RICE
Serves 4-6

Rice is a big staple in many homes, but since I have never been a big rice eater, I wanted to create a simple recipe that not only my family would love but that I would enjoy also. If you let the bottom burn a little, that is called razpa (yummy) and you can also fry some eggs and add to the top pf the rice and that's called montado al caballo. This rice recipe is a sure way to get anyone to eat rice.

- 2 cups long grain rice (Mahatma)
- 2 ½ cups water
- 6 cloves garlic (minced)
- 1 tablespoon olive oil
- ½ tablespoon. salt

1. Add the rice to a medium sauce pan and clean the rice 5 times. (I do this to prevent clumping and the surface starches, but it's optional)

2. After the rice has been cleaned, add the final 2 ½ cups water, garlic, salt and olive oil and stir.
3. Place the pan on stove to high heat
4. When the water starts to boil, cover the pan and lower the heat to medium for 15 minutes
5. Fluff the rice with a fork and lower the heat to the lowest setting and cover until ready to serve

MUSHROOM GARLIC RICE
Serves 4-6

I invented this recipe simply to add a little umph to the rice and also to give it more substance if it was to stand alone as a meal.

- Recipe of garlic rice (page 54)
- 2 large Portobello mushrooms caps – medium dice
- 2 cloves garlic - minced
- 2 tablespoon olive oil
- 1 ½ teaspoon salt
- 1 teaspoon pepper

1. While the garlic rice is being cooked make the mushroom mix
2. In a large non-stick sauté pan on medium heat add the olive oil and the mushrooms and start sautéing
3. Add salt and pepper and cook for about 2 minutes
4. Add the garlic and cook for another 2 minutes
5. Stir the mushrooms into the rice and serve

ROASTED GARLIC SPROUTS

Serves 4-6

I absolutely love Brussel sprouts, especially when some of the leaves get crispy from cooking them. I have had them in a few different styles, but my favorite is roasting them. I wanted to make something a little different then just roasted sprouts and since I love roasted garlic, I figured, why not mix them together.

- 1 ½ pounds Brussel sprouts (cut in half)
- 8 cloves garlic (whole and wrapped in foil)
- 1 Vidalia onion (sliced thin)
- 1 ½ teaspoon salt
- 1 teaspoon pepper
- ¼ cup olive oil

1. In a preheated 450 degrees oven add the garlic and roast for about 20 minutes. Once the garlic is ready, take out of the foil and turn into a paste.
2. In a large bowl, mix the Brussel sprouts with ½ of the oil, salt and pepper well. Place on a baking sheet in a single layer and add to the same 450-degree oven for about 30 – 35 minutes.
3. In a medium sauté pan on medium heat add ¼ of the remaining oil and the onion and cook until a little golden, but not caramelized. Remove from heat.
4. When the sprouts are ready, remove from the oven and place in the same bowl. Add the garlic, the rest of the oil and the onion mixture and mix well. Sprinkle with salt and pepper if needed.

SPICY GREEN BEANS

Serves 4

Ever since my son became a vegetarian, I have been able to kill two birds with one stone. Not only am I creating delicious vegetarian dishes, but my daughter is trying all sorts of vegetables and starting to like them; this is one of her favorites of all the veggie dishes

- 1 pound of fresh French cut green beans
- 4 cloves garlic (minced)
- 2 tablespoons olive oil
- ½ tablespoon red pepper flakes
- ¼ teaspoon Kosher salt
- ⅛ teaspoon pepper
- 2 tablespoons low sodium soy sauce
- 2 tablespoon apple cider vinegar
- 2 tablespoons corn starch
- 1 tablespoon white sugar

1. In a medium sauce pan on high heat add the green beans and fill with water enough to cover the beans
2. Bring to a boil and cook for about 2 minutes
3. Remove the green beans and add them to a bowl filled with ice water to stop cooking and then drain and pat dry the green beans
4. Mix together the soy sauce, corn starch, vinegar and sugar and make a sauce
5. In a large skillet on medium heat add the oil and garlic and sauté for about 2-3 minutes
6. Add the red pepper flakes, salt, pepper and sauce and bring to a boil and then reduce heat to low and add the green beans and cook through while moving around the beans until the sauce thickens

ZUCCHINI PARMESAN PANCAKES

Serves 4-6

Waffles and pancakes are such a staple brunch menu and they usually are accompanied with something sweet. I like sweets, but I love savory so one day I decided to make a savory waffle. These waffles are so tasty I have even used them as the bread for a sandwich. You can also use this recipe and make pancakes instead.

- 1 ½ cup all-purpose flour
- 3 ½ teaspoon baking powder
- 1 teaspoon Kosher salt
- ½ teaspoon pepper
- 1 teaspoon dry parsley
- 1 teaspoon garlic powder

- 1 ¼ cup milk
- 1 egg
- 1 cup shredded zucchini (drain moister out with a cheese cloth)
- 3 tablespoon butter (melted)
- ½ cup freshly grated parmesan cheese

1. Add the flour, baking powder, salt, pepper, garlic powder and dry parsley in a bowl and whisk together
2. Add the milk, butter and egg and mix well until all the dry ingredients have been blended
3. Stir in the zucchini and parmesan cheese
4. In a large non-stick pan on medium high heat, place about ¼ cup of batter and cook until golden brown on each side
5. You can cook about 4 pancakes at a time

ZUCCHINI PARMESAN PANCAKES

As you see by my selection in recipes a main course can be breakfast, lunch, dinner and my favorite...brunch.

main course

Asian Pork Burger
Asian Veggie Burger
Café con Leche Pancakes
Camarones Enchilada al Caribe
Churrasco Fried Rice
Coconut Shrimp
Cuban Philly with Mojo
Fricassee de Pollo
Quiches
   Italian
   Veggie
   Caramelized Onion and Bacon

el plato fuerte

Italian Omelet
Linguine a la Carbonara
Picadillo
Pollo a la Duquesa
Seared Hog Snapper with Salsa
Seared Corvina with Lemon Butter
Shrimp Scampi
Pollo a la Plancha
Seared Salmon with Soy Butter
Vaca Frita
Veggie burger

ASIAN PORK BURGER

Serves 4

Since this is the Diversified table and I have some carnivores in the house, I made this recipe for them. This is a great way not to always have to make an entirely different meal.

- 1 pound of ground pork
- 1 cup Shitake mushrooms (diced)
- 2 cloves garlic (minced)
- 1 green onion (diced small)
- 2 tablespoons sesame seeds
- 1 teaspoon kosher salt
- ½ teaspoon pepper
- 1 teaspoon garlic powder
- 1 teaspoon onion powder
- 1 teaspoon cumin
- 1 teaspoon turmeric
- ½ teaspoon ground ginger
- 1 tablespoon soy sauce
- ¾ cup all-purpose flour
- 1 egg (beaten)
- 4 basil leaves (chopped)
- 2 tablespoon olive oil
- 4 multigrain burger buns

1. In a small non-stick pan, add ½ of the oil and on medium heat, cook the mushroom and garlic. Cook for about 1-2 minutes and then remove from heat and let cool.
2. Mix the rest of the ingredients (except the buns) into the pork and make sure that it is all incorporated well.
3. Add the mushroom and garlic mixture and mix well.
4. Make 4 patties and refrigerate for about 30 minutes to firm up.
5. In a large non-stick pan heat the rest of the oil on medium high heat and cook the burgers, about 4-5 minutes on each side.
6. Remove from the pan and place each patty on its own bun.
7. You can top it with any condiments you like.

ASIAN VEGGIE BURGER

Serves 4

I made this for my son and his girlfriend both vegetarians. I am always buying them different frozen veggie patties and I felt it would only be beneficial to my ego for me to make my own. Well, they gave me the thumbs up and here it is for you.

- 1 can Garbanzo Beans (drained and rinsed)
- 1 cup Shitake mushrooms (diced)
- 2 cloves garlic (minced)
- 1 green onion (diced small)
- 2 tablespoons sesame seeds
- 1 teaspoon kosher salt
- ½ teaspoon pepper
- 1 teaspoon garlic powder
- 1 teaspoon onion powder
- 1 teaspoon cumin
- 1 teaspoon turmeric
- ½ teaspoon ground ginger
- 1 tablespoon soy sauce
- ¾ cup all-purpose flour
- 1 egg (beaten)
- 2 tablespoon flat leaf parsley (chopped)
- 2 tablespoon olive oil
- 4 multigrain burger buns

1. Smash the garbanzos with a fork, leave whatever consistency you like. I personally like it a little coarse.
2. In a small non-stick pan, add ½ of the oil and on medium heat, cook the mushroom and garlic. Cook for about 1-2 minutes and then remove from heat and let cool.
3. Mix the rest of the ingredients (except the buns) with the garbanzos and make sure that it is all incorporated well.
4. Add the mushroom and garlic mixture and mix well.
5. Make 4 patties and refrigerate for about 30 minutes to firm up.
6. In a large non-stick pan heat the rest of the oil on medium high heat and cook the burgers, about 2-3 minutes on each side.
7. Remove from the pan and place each patty on its own bun.
8. You can top it with any condiments you like.

ASIAN VEGGIE BURGER

CAFÉ CON LECHE PANCAKES

Serves 4-6

My daughter loves café con leche and toast for breakfast and she also love pancakes so I put them together and came up with this recipe.

- 2 cup Flour
- 2 ½ teaspoon baking powder
- 1 teaspoon salt
- 4 tablespoon brown sugar
- 2 Eggs
- 3 tablespoon melted unsalted butter

- 4 tablespoon Instant coffee (I use Bustelo)
- 1 ¼ cup milk
- Non-stick spray
- Sauce
- 14 ounce can Condensed milk
- 2 table spoons milk

1. Whisk together the flour, baking powder, salt and sugar in a large bowl (3 quarts)
2. In a separate bowl, beat the butter, eggs and milk
3. Add the instant coffee to the liquid mixture and mix until dissolved
4. Make a well in the middle of the dry mixture and pour the liquid mixture and stir well until everything is incorporated
5. In a large non-stick skillet (12") on medium heat, spray some non-stick spray or melt some butter and pour some of the pancake batter (about 4-6-inch diameter in size)
6. Try to add 2 pancakes at a time (if possible)
7. When the pancake batter starts to bubble (about 2-3 minutes), flip with a spatula to cook the other side (about 1 more minute)
8. Remove from heat and place on a plate
9. Mix the condensed milk and regular milk together and serve

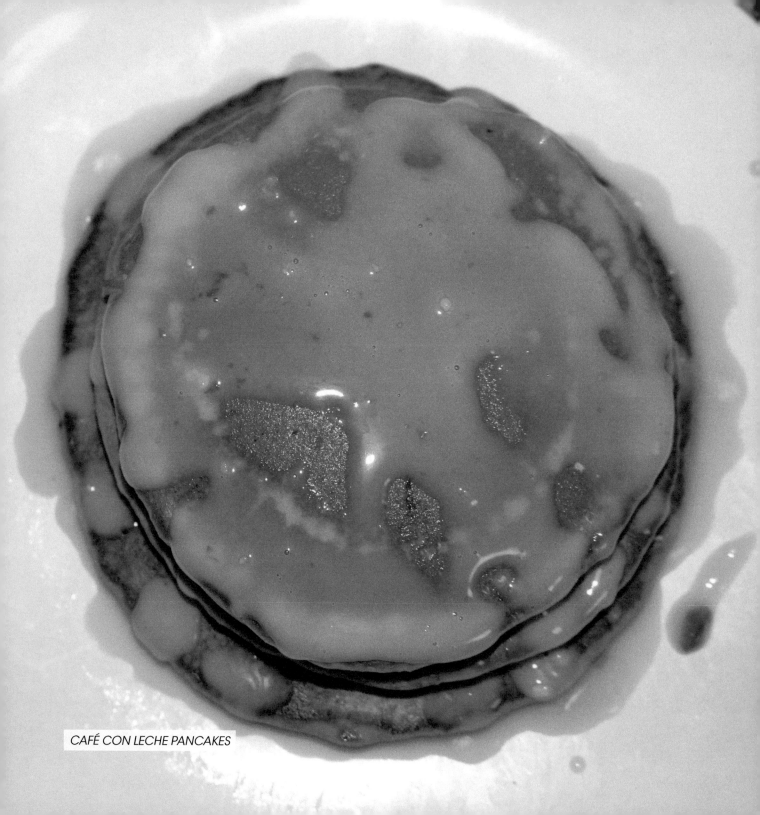

CAFÉ CON LECHE PANCAKES

CAMARONES ENCHILADO AL CARIBE

Serves 4-6

This is probably the recipe that I have cooked the most since I started writing the book. It's changed a bit as I have been perfecting it, but originally, I wrote it around an herb that a friend of mine made herself. She would grow a specific pepper and then dry and ground it. I have removed the herb from the recipe because she no longer makes it, but that doesn't matter, the recipe is the best.

- 2 pounds, high-quality, raw large shrimp (peeled and deveined)
- 1 red pepper (small dice)
- 1 orange pepper (small dice)
- 1 yellow pepper (small dice)
- 1 small Vidalia onion (small dice)
- 3 cloves of garlic (minced)
- 2-3 tablespoons of tomato paste (alternative is tomato sauce – 8 ounce can)

- ½ teaspoon cumin
- ½ teaspoon turmeric
- ½ teaspoon smoked paprika
- ½ teaspoon kosher salt
- ¼ teaspoon pepper
- 2 bay leaves
- ⅛ – ¼ teaspoon red pepper flakes
- 2 tablespoons of freshly chopped cilantro
- 3 tablespoons olive oil

1. In a large Dutch oven on medium heat add 2 tablespoons of olive oil, onion, red, orange and yellow peppers and cook until onions are translucent (about 5-6 minutes)
2. Add the garlic and cook for about 2 more minutes
3. Add the rest of the olive oil and tomato paste and stir well until the vegetables are well coated
4. Add the cumin, turmeric, smoked paprika, salt, pepper, pepper flakes and stir well then add the bay leaves
5. Reduce the heat to low, cover and simmer for about 15 – 20 minutes
6. Raise the temperature to medium low heat and add the shrimp and cilantro. Cook until the shrimp are pink (about 10 - 15 minutes)
7. Remove the bay leaves before serving

CHURRASCO FRIED RICE

Serves 4-6

Well my daughter loves to steak and churrasco is one of her favorites. She also loves rice, especially rice with soy sauce. Soooooo, I made this recipe. It is the best of both worlds, Latin and Asian flavors.

- 2 cups of garlic rice (recipe on page 54)
- 1-pound Churrasco (skirt steak) seasoned with salt and pepper and sliced into ½ inch pieces
- 2 tablespoons olive oil
- 2 carrots (small dice)
- 2 celery stalks (thin slices)
- 1 Vidalia onion (small dice)
- 1 red pepper (small dice)
- 1 green pepper (small dice)
- 3 cloves of garlic (minced)
- 3 eggs (beaten)
- 2 tablespoons sesame seeds
- ¼ tablespoon onion powder
- ¼ tablespoon garlic powder
- ¼ tablespoon kosher salt
- ⅛ tablespoon pepper
- ¼ cup Soy sauce
- 2 tablespoons of unsalted butter
- 1 tablespoon lemon juice
- 2 tablespoons of cilantro (chopped)
- 3 scallions (both white and green part diced)

1. In a large sauté pan or wok on medium high heat, add the olive oil, onion, carrot and celery and cook until the onion is translucent (about 5-6 minutes)
2. Add the garlic and cook for about 2 more minutes
3. Remove the vegetable mix and keep in a separate bowl for later
4. Add the skirt steak to the pan and sear until desired temperature (I like medium rare)
5. Add the rice, vegetable mix, sesame seeds, onion and garlic powder, salt and pepper to the pan and mix well with the steak
6. Make a well in the middle of the pan and add the egg. Allow the egg to scramble and mix into the rice
7. Add the soy sauce and lemon juice, mix then add the butter, cilantro and scallions and continue to mix until everything is well incorporated

COCONUT SHRIMP

Serves 4

Coconut happens to be one of my favorite flavors and I would add it to everything if I could. So naturally I had to add it to shrimp. This recipe can be found in many restaurants and the secret, I believe, is the size of the shrimp, the larger the better.

- 25-30 large shrimp – cleaned and deveined
- ⅓ cup all-purpose flour
- 1 cup sweetened shredded coconut
- 1 teaspoon salt
- ¾ cup panko breading
- ½ teaspoon pepper
- 1 teaspoon dry parsley
- 2 large eggs – beaten
- 2 - 3 cups of vegetable oil

1. Add the oil to a medium skillet on medium high heat
2. Combine the flour, salt, pepper and parsley in a bowl
3. In a different bowl place, the beaten eggs
4. In a third bowl place the panko and the coconut
5. Take each shrimp, one at a time and dip into the flour, then the egg and then the coconut mixture
6. Before you add the first shrimp, lower the heat to medium
7. Cook each shrimp on each side until golden brown
8. Place the shrimp on a plate lined with towel paper, to soak the oil and then place on a separate plate

COCONUT SHRIMP

CUBAN PHILLY

Serves 4

I think that pork tenderloin is such a great cut meat (and inexpensive) that I always have it around. One day, my husband and I were in the mood for a sandwich (before I gave up meat) and the pork is all I had along with the rest the ingredients and voila the Cuban Philly was born.

- 1 whole pork tenderloin (about 2 pounds - slice into 8-10 slices)
- 1 cup mojo – (recipe to follow)
- 1 Vidalia Onion (sliced julienne)
- Kosher salt and pepper
- 1 tablespoon olive oil
- 4 Cuban breads (6 inches long)
- 8 slices provolone cheese
- 1 green plantain (shredded)
- 2 cups vegetable oil

Mojo
- ⅓ cup olive oil
- 6-8 cloves garlic (minced)
- ½ cup on Vidalia Onion (small dice)
- ⅔ cups orange juice
- ⅓ cup lime juice
- ½ teaspoon cumin
- 1 teaspoon kosher salt
- ½ teaspoon pepper
- ½ cup freshly chopped cilantro

1. In a small sauce pan on medium high heat add the vegetable oil and fry the green plantain in batches then set aside on a plate lined with paper towel to drain excess oil and sprinkle some salt while still hot
2. Place the tenderloins in a Ziploc bag and add the mojo, then place in the refrigerator for about 2-3 hours, remove from the bag and discard the mojo then sprinkle with salt and pepper
3. In a 12" sauté pan on medium high heat, add ½ the olive oil and onions and cook until translucent (7-8 minutes) and remove from the pan
4. Let the pan rise to temperature again (about 1 minute) then add the rest the olive oil and cook the pork until desired temperature (I like medium to medium well – about 2-3 minutes on each side)
5. Remove the pork and let rest
6. Add the 2-3 slices (depending on the size) to the bread and then top with the cooked onions

7. If you have extra fresh mojo, you can pour a little on the onions
8. Place 2 slices provolone over the onions and place on a baking sheet
9. Place in the broiler for about 1 – 2 minutes (just enough to melt the cheese and not burn the bread)
10. Top with the fried tostones

MOJO

1. You can add mojo to many different dishes as a sauce or use it as a marinade. Another very common dish is yucca con mojo which you will find the recipe in this cookbook.
2. In a small sauce pan add the olive oil, garlic, onion, cumin, salt and pepper and cook on medium low heat for about 10 minutes
3. Remove from the heat and add the orange juice, lime juice and cilantro
4. Refrigerate (good for about 5 days)

FRICASSEE DE POLLO

Serves 4 - 6

This is a staple in my home and probably in any Cuban family home. Sofrito, is the typical base for many Cuban dishes. The great thing about a base is that you can change it up a little here and there if you want

- 8 chicken thighs (I use boneless and skinless)
- 1 Vidalia onion (medium dice)
- 1 red pepper (medium dice)
- 3 cloves garlic (minced)
- 1 tablespoon olive oil
- 2 tablespoons tomato sauce
- ¼ teaspoon cumin
- ¼ teaspoon smoked paprika
- ¼ teaspoon turmeric
- ¼ teaspoon onion powder
- ¼ teaspoon garlic powder
- ¼ teaspoon kosher salt
- ⅛ teaspoon pepper
- 2 bay leaves
- 1 tablespoon chopped parsley
- Spanish green olives (about 20 – whole or sliced)

1. In a large non-stick fry pan on medium high heat, sear the chicken with a little salt and pepper until golden brown on each side but not cooked through (about 2 – 3 minutes on each side and set aside
2. In a medium or large Dutch oven on medium heat, add the olive oil, onions and red pepper and sauté until onions are translucent (about 5-6 minutes)
3. Add the garlic and cook for another 1-2 minutes
4. Add the tomato sauce, cumin, smoked paprika, onion and garlic powder, turmeric, salt and pepper and stir well
5. Nestle the chicken in the pan and make sure that it is covered with some of the sauce
6. Add the olives and the bay leaves, lower the heat to low and simmer for about 30 – 40 minutes
7. Remove the bay leaves and add the parsley and stir before serving

FRICASSEE DE POLLO

ITALIAN OMELET

Serves 2

I love going to breakfast, especially when I am on vacation. When my husband and I went to San Francisco for my 35th birthday we visited this fantastic restaurant. I ordered the Italian omelet and loved it so much I had to make my own version when I got home.

- 6 eggs
- 2 tablespoons of tomatoes (small dice)
- 2 tablespoons Vidalia onion (small dice)
- 1 garlic clove (minced)
- 1 tablespoon of pesto
- 3 tablespoons freshly grated parmesan cheese
- 3 tablespoons cooked chicken breast (small dice)
- Salt and pepper to taste
- Non-stick spray

1. Place the eggs in a medium bowl, add salt and pepper and beat well with a whisk
2. Place a medium non-stick pan on medium heat and add non-stick spray to the bottom of the pan
3. Add the onion and garlic and cook for about 4-5 minutes
4. Add the tomato, chicken and pesto to the mix and stir well
5. Add the eggs and cook the egg through
6. Add the parmesan cheese to the middle and fold the egg over
7. Cut in half and serve

LINGUINE A LA CARBONARA

Serves 4-6

This is my husband's absolute favorite dish. He would always tell me about a restaurant that served the best carbonara he has ever had. Well, that was a challenge and I knew that I had to learn how to make this dish.

- 2 pounds of linguine
- 1 Vidalia onion (medium dice)
- 2 cloves garlic (minced)
- 16 ounces of bacon or pancetta (sliced thin)
- 2 eggs
- ½ cup heavy cream

- 2 tablespoon cream cheese
- ½ teaspoon Kosher salt for sauce
- 1 tablespoon Kosher salt for water
- ¼ teaspoon pepper
- 1 tablespoon flat leaf parsley (chopped)
- 1 cup freshly grated parmesan cheese

1. In a large stock pot add 7 – 8 cups water and 1 tablespoon salt and bring to a boil
2. Add the pasta and cook for 10 minutes until al dente then drain
3. In a large sauté pan on medium heat add bacon and render until almost fully cooked
4. With the same oil from the bacon add the onion and cook until translucent, about 4-5 minutes
5. Add the garlic and cook for another 1-2 minutes
6. Add the pasta to the bacon add the salt, pepper, heavy cream and cream cheese and mix well
7. Remove from the heat and add the eggs one at a time while blending into the pasta
8. Add the parsley and cheese and mix before serving

QUICHES

Serves 6-8

Quiches are one of the most popular things that I make for brunch and according to my mother-in-law, they are her favorite. Quiches are such a great way to get a lot of flavors in a pie shape that easy to serve and to carry when you are with food. Below are several quiche recipes that have been the most popular of all the ones I have made

ITALIAN QUICHE

- 4 eggs
- 1 cup milk
- 1 teaspoon Kosher salt
- ½ teaspoon pepper
- ½ teaspoon garlic powder
- ½ teaspoon dry oregano

- 1 chicken breast (cooked and medium dice)
- ½ cup red onion (small dice)
- ¼ cup tomato (small dice)
- 1 cup shredded mozzarella cheese
- ⅓ cup shredded parmesan cheese
- Ready-made pie crust

1. Preheat oven to 400 degrees
2. Poke some holes with a fork on the bottom of the pie crust and cook for about 10 minutes then remove from heat at let rest, lower the oven heat to 375 degrees
3. In a medium bowl add the eggs, milk, salt, pepper, garlic powder and oregano then beat with a whisk well
4. Layer the chicken on the bottom of the pie crust and make sure that it covers the entire bottom of the pie
5. Layer the onion, then tomatoes, then mozzarella on top of the chicken
6. Pour the egg mixture all over the pie (try not to let the mixture flow out from the sides)
7. Top the pie with the parmesan cheese and bake for 35-40 minutes or until the mixture is firm
8. Remove from the heat and let cool for about 10 minutes and serve

VEGGIE QUICHE

- 4 eggs
- 1 cup milk
- 1 teaspoon Kosher salt
- ½ teaspoon pepper
- ½ teaspoon garlic powder
- ½ teaspoon dry parsley
- ½ cup sliced cremini mushrooms
- ½ cup Vidalia onion (medium dice)
- ½ cup frozen spinach (thawed and drained)
- ½ cup red pepper (small dice)
- 1 cup shredded swiss cheese
- Ready-made pie crust

1. Preheat oven to 400 degrees
2. Poke some holes with a fork on the bottom of the pie crust and cook for about 10 minutes then remove from heat at let rest, lower the oven heat to 375 degrees
3. In a medium bowl add the eggs, milk, salt, pepper, garlic powder and parsley then beat with a whisk well
4. Layer the spinach on the bottom of the pie crust and make sure that it covers most of the bottom of the pie
5. Layer the mushrooms, pepper, onion then swiss cheese on top of the spinach
6. Pour the egg mixture all over the pie (try not to let the mixture flow out from the sides)
7. Bake for 35-40 minutes or until the mixture is firm
8. Remove from the heat and let cool for about 10 minutes and serve

CARAMELIZED ONION AND BACON QUICHE

- 4 eggs
- 1 cup milk
- 1 teaspoon Kosher salt
- ½ teaspoon pepper
- ½ teaspoon dry parsley
- 2 Vidalia onions (sliced thin)
- 1 tablespoon olive oil
- 1 cup cooked bacon (chopped)
- 1 cup shredded gouda cheese
- Ready-made pie crust

1. In a non-stick medium sauté pan on medium heat cook onions until caramelized, but don't burn (about 20-30 minutes)
2. Preheat oven to 400 degrees
3. Poke some holes with a fork on the bottom of the pie crust and cook for about 10 minutes then remove from heat at let rest, lower the oven heat to 375 degrees

4. In a medium bowl add the eggs, milk, salt, pepper and parsley then beat with a whisk well
5. Layer the onions on the bottom of the pie crust and make sure that it covers the entire bottom of the pie
6. Layer all the bacon and then the gouda on top of the onions
7. Pour the egg mixture all over the pie (try not to let the mixture flow out from the sides)
8. Bake for 35-40 minutes or until the mixture is firm
9. Remove from the heat and let cool for about 10 minutes and serve

PICADILLO

Serves 4-6

This is another staple in a Cuban home and a different little change to the sofrito. I also use this recipe in the pastelitos de carne that are delicious.

- 1 pound of ground beef (90/10 if not it gets too greasy)
- 1 Vidalia onion (small dice)
- 1 green pepper (small dice)
- 3 cloves of garlic (minced)
- 2 tablespoons tomato sauce
- ¼ teaspoon of cumin
- ¼ teaspoon of onion powder
- ¼ teaspoon of garlic powder
- ¼ teaspoon smoked paprika
- ¼ teaspoon of turmeric
- ¼ teaspoon of salt
- 1/8 teaspoon of pepper
- Green olives (about 20 - whole or chopped)
- 2 bay leaves
- 1 tablespoon Olive oil
- 1 tablespoon chopped of cilantro

1. In a medium or large Dutch oven on medium heat, add the olive oil, onions and green pepper and sauté until onions are translucent (about 5-6 minutes)
2. Add the garlic and cook for another 1-2 minutes
3. Add the meat and cook until almost brown
4. Add the tomato sauce, cumin, smoked paprika, onion and garlic powder, turmeric, salt and pepper and stir well
5. Add the olives and the bay leaves, lower the heat to low and simmer for about 20 - 30 minutes
6. Remove the bay leaves and add the cilantro and stir before serving

POLLO A LA DUQUESA

Serves 4-6

When I was pregnant with my daughter I craved this dish from a small restaurant in Miami that my husband and I used to frequent. However, I was living in Naples, Florida. I craved it so much that I decided to make my own version. Thank goodness that I did because the restaurant closed a few years later.

- 8-10 chicken thighs (skinless and boneless)
- 1 ½ cup chicken stock
- 1 cup sliced button mushrooms
- 1 cup Vidalia onion (large dice)
- ½ cup green pepper (large dice)
- 3 cloves garlic (minced)
- 4 tablespoon flour
- 1 tablespoon olive oil
- 1 teaspoon red wine vinegar
- ¼ teaspoon kosher salt (extra to season the chicken)
- ⅛ teaspoon pepper (extra to season the chicken)
- 10-15 large shrimp (cleaned and deveined, tail off)

1. In a large Dutch oven on medium high heat add the oil
2. Season the chicken with salt and pepper on both sides
3. Sear the chicken until golden brown on both sides
4. Remove the chicken from the pan and place on a separate plate
5. Add the onion and the green pepper and cook until onion is translucent, about 4-5 minutes
6. Add the garlic and the mushrooms and cook for another 2-3 minutes
7. Add the salt and pepper
8. Spread the flour over the vegetables and stir well then add the stock and vinegar and stir again
9. Bring to a boil and then reduce the heat
10. Add the chicken back to the pan cover and cook for about 20 minutes
11. Add the shrimp and cook until pink, about 5-6 minutes, don't over cook

POLLO A LA PLANCHA

Serves 4 - 6

This is a safe haven dish and can be eaten alone with a side dish or can be sliced and added to a salad. You can also make this into a sandwich on Cuban bread with a little mojo.

- 4 skinless chicken breasts (butterflied)
- 1 Vidalia onion (sliced thin)
- 1 tablespoon lime juice
- ½ tablespoon flat leaf parsley

- 1 tablespoon olive oil
- Kosher salt to season
- Pepper to season

1. Wrap chicken breast with plastic wrap
2. Pound the chicken until it is ½ inch think and repeat until all the chicken has been pounded
3. Season the chicken on both sides with salt and pepper
4. In a large skillet on medium high heat add the oil
5. Sear the chicken on both sides until golden brown
6. Remove from the heat and set to the side
7. Add the onion and parsley to the same pan and cook until translucent and a little golden brown, about 3-4 minutes
8. Remove from the heat and stir in the lime juice to deglaze the pan

SEARED HOG SNAPPER
with salsa
Serves 2

The first time I ate Hog Snapper was at a Peruvian restaurant my husband and I used to go to in 1998. It was delicious! Now that I am a pescatarian, I am always trying to make fish recipes that I want to eat all the time, this is one of them.

- 2 Hog Snapper Fillets (cleaned, skin off)
- 1 ½ tablespoon olive oil
- Flour to dust the fish
- ½ cup tomato (small dice)
- 1 cup yellow pepper (small dice)

- ½ Vidalia onion (small dice)
- 1 clove garlic (minced)
- ½ teaspoon dry oregano
- ¼ teaspoon kosher salt (a little for the flour and a little for the salsa)
- ⅛ teaspoon pepper (a little for the flour and a little for the salsa)

1. In a large non-stick fry pan on medium high heat, add ½ tablespoon olive oil and sauté the onion, tomato, yellow pepper, garlic, salt, pepper and oregano (about 3-4 minutes)
2. Remove from the pan and let sit on a separate plate
3. Dust the snapper with flour, salt and pepper
4. In the same large non-stick fry pan on medium high heat, add the rest of the olive oil and pan fry the fillets until golden brown (about 2-3 minutes on each side)
5. Remove the fish from the pan and serve with the salsa on top

SEARED CORVINA
with lemon butter
Serves 4

Corvina is a very white fish, which I love and is not very common to find. I was at the fish market one day and when my husband saw it he told me I had to buy it and make something delicious. I try to make my fish recipes simple and this recipe, though simple, packs a punch.

- 1 pound corvina
- 1 tablespoon oil
- ½ cup of white wine
- ¼ cup lemon juice
- ½ cup Vidalia onion (very small dice)

- 3 cloves garlic (minced)
- 5 tablespoons butter
- ¼ teaspoon sea salt
- ⅛ teaspoon pepper
- ¼ teaspoon dry parsley

1. In a non-stick skillet on medium high heat add oil
2. Sear the corvina until golden brown on both sides, about 3-4 minutes each side
3. In a nonstick medium sauté pan on medium heat add the wine, lemon juice, onion and garlic and cook for about 2 minutes
4. Add the salt, pepper and dry parsley to pan and cook for another 2 minutes
5. Add the butter and mix with a whisk and lower the heat to low and cook for about 2 more minutes
6. Pour the sauce over the fish and serve

SEARED CORVINA WITH LEMON BUTTER SAUCE

SEARED SALMON
with soy butter
Serves 4

This is one of the simplest recipes I have in the book, but it is so tasty. It is also the way I finally got my daughter to try and love salmon for the first time.

- 4 – 6-ounce fillets of salmon (skin on or off)
- 1 tablespoon salt
- ½ tablespoon pepper
- 1 tablespoon olive oil
- 4 ounces salted butter
- 1 tablespoon soy sauce (low sodium)
- 2 tablespoon flat leaf parsley (rough chop)

1. Season salmon with salt and pepper on both sides
2. In a large non-stick skillet on medium high heat add the oil
3. Sear the salmon top side down and cook until golden brown
4. Flip salmon and cook the other side until golden brown or until the skin is crispy
   a. Medium rare (2-3 minutes each side)
   b. Medium (3-4 minutes each side)
   c. Well (4-5 minutes each side)
5. Remove the salmon from the pan and add the butter, soy and parsley until butter is melted
6. Pour over the salmon

SEARED SALMON WITH SOY BUTTER SAUCE

SHRIMP SCAMPI

Serves 4-6

Since I became a pescatarian I make a lot of shrimp dishes and this is one of my favorites. I have ordered this dish in many restaurants and have seen it made in a few different ways but none the less they are always very tasty.

- 1 ½ pounds medium shrimp — about 60 shrimp (peeled, deveined and tail off)
- 2 shallots (cut in half and sliced thin)
- 10 cloves of garlic (sliced thin)
- 8 tablespoons unsalted butter (1 stick cut in 4 pieces)
- 4 tablespoon olive oil

- 1 tablespoon lemon juice
- ½ lemon sliced thin
- ⅓ cup flat leaf parsley (chopped)
- ½ teaspoon Kosher salt
- ¼ teaspoon white pepper
- ⅛ teaspoon fresh ginger (minced)

1. In a large deep non-stick pan sauté pan on medium heat add the oil
2. Add shallots, garlic and ginger and cook for about 2-3 minutes
3. Add the butter, lemon juice, salt and pepper and cook another 3-4 minutes
4. Add the shrimp and lemon slices and cook for until pink, about 5-6 minutes
5. Add the parsley stir and serve

VACA FRITA

Serves 4-6

Before my son became a vegetarian, this was his most requested dish, however, it remains one of my husband's favorites. This is a pretty simple dish that packs a huge punch and most of it should be made in advance.

- 2 pounds of flank steak (falda)
- 2 Vidalia onions (thinly sliced)
- 6 cloves of garlic (minced)
- 1 tablespoon Kosher salt
- ½ tablespoon pepper
- 2 limes
- 1 tablespoon olive oil

1. In a large Dutch oven on high heat add the meat and fill with enough water to cover the meat
2. Bring to a boil and cook the meat for about 20 – 25 minutes
3. Take off the heat and let cool in the refrigerator
4. When cool enough to the touch, shred the meat and place in a large bowl
5. Season with salt and pepper
6. Add the onion and the garlic to the meat and mix so it is evenly distributed
7. In a large skillet on medium high heat add oil
8. Sear the meat and onion mixture in batches until the meat is crispy but still a little tender
9. Once all the meat is cooked serve with lime wedges and garlic rice

VACA FRITA

VEGGIE BURGER

Serves 4-6

I created this recipe for my burger restaurant in 2009 and it was one m=of my best sellers. I have had many veggie burgers and this one is one of my favorites

- 1 cup green lentils (rinsed)
- ¼ cup pearl barley
- ½ cup of cooked corn kernels
- 1 cup Vidalia onion (small dice)
- 1 garlic clove (minced)
- ½ teaspoon cumin
- 1 teaspoon curry
- ½ teaspoon Kosher salt (plus a little more)
- ¼ teaspoon pepper

- 3 tablespoon fresh flat leaf parsley
- 1 cup bread crumbs
- 6 slices of Havarti cheese (optional)
- 1 egg (beaten)
- 1 tablespoon unsalted butter
- 2 tablespoon olive oil
- 6 onion buns
- 2 tablespoons honey mustard

1. In a medium sauce pan on medium high heat, add the lentil and barley and add enough water to cover by about 2 inches
2. Add some salt to the water and bring to a boil then reduce the heat and simmer until tender, about 20-30 minutes then drain and set aside to cool
3. In a medium skillet on medium heat, add the butter and onion and cook until tender, about 3-4 minutes then add the garlic, cumin and curry and cook for another 1-2 minutes
4. Set aside in a bowl and allow to cool
5. Mix in the lentil mix with the onion mix and add the parsley, salt, pepper, egg and bread crumbs and mix well until all the ingredients have been incorporated
6. In a food processor, pure about 1 cup of the mixture and then fold back into the mixture
7. Place in the refrigerator for about an hour then mold into 6 patties
8. In a large skillet on medium high heat add the olive oil and sear each patty until golden brown on one side (about 2 minutes) then flip add the cheese (optional) and cook about another 2 minutes and the cheese is melted
9. Serve on the onion bun with honey mustard

Dessert doesn't really need an introduction does it? I could have made this section larger than it is, but since I must practice on all the recipes to perfect them, felt I should not go crazy

dessert

Arroz con Leche Brule
Cacao Tres Leches
Coconut Rum Cake
Dulce de Leche Flan
Flan de Cacao

poster

Guava and Cream Cheese Ice Cream
Key Lime Pie Ice Cream
Popcorn and Sno-Cap Ice Cream

ARROZ CON LECHE BRULEE

Serves 4

As you can see, many of the recipes throughout the cookbook call for rice as a side dish, so naturally it wouldn't be complete if I didn't have a dessert with rice. My husband and I had a similar dessert once at a restaurant and I thought it was such a great idea, so this is my version.

- 1 cup long grain white rice (I use Mahatma)
- 5 cups of water
- 1 Cinnamon stick
- 14 ounce can of condensed milk
- 2 1/2 cup of milk (whole milk is best, but you can use what you have in the fridge)
- ½ tablespoon vanilla extract
- 4 tablespoons white sugar

1. In a medium heavy saucepan on medium high heat add water and bring to boil the water
2. Add the rice and cinnamon stick, lower to medium heat and cook the rice until tender, about 15-18 minutes stirring often
3. Drain the water and discard the cinnamon stick
4. In the same saucepan on medium heat, stir in the milk, condensed milk and vanilla extract
5. Bring back to a quick boil then reduce the heat to low and simmer for about 15 -20 minutes until the rice has a creamy consistency (continue stirring so the bottom does not burn
6. Cook until thick making sure to continue stirring and cook for about 20 more minutes
7. Distribute in single serving dishes (make sure they are heat resistant)
8. Dust the top of each dish with sugar evenly and place in the refrigerator for about 1 hour
9. Place in the broiler (high) until sugar melts and turns brown (if you have a torch, you can use that instead)

CACAO TRES LECHES

Serves 8-12

Huge fan of this dessert. There is something about a moist cake in a delicious milky sauce that really gets me. I am usually not the dessert type and if I do it's usually more of chocolate love affair, but this one is good!

Cake
- 1 cup all-purpose flour
- 1 ½ teaspoon baking powder
- ¼ teaspoon Kosher salt
- 5 large eggs – split whites and yolk
- 1 cup sugar
- ⅓ cup milk
- 1 teaspoon vanilla extract

Leche
- ¼ cup heavy cream
- 14 ounce can of condensed milk
- 12 ounce can evaporated milk

Merengue
- 2 cups heavy whipping cream
- 3 tablespoon sugar
- 2 tablespoons cacao powder

1. Preheat oven to 350 degrees
2. With a stick of butter, grease a 9 x 13-inch cake pan by just rubbing it around the pan
3. In a large bowl, sift the flour, baking powder and salt (I use a medium strainer)
4. With a hand-held mixer, beat the yolks and ¾ cup of the sugar until the eggs look pale, then stir in the milk and the vanilla extract
5. Pour the egg yolk mix with the flour and stir well but gently
6. Beat the egg white on high speed until soft peaks and then add the rest of the sugar and beat until stiff peaks
7. Gently fold the egg whites into the flour batter until combined then pour into the cake pan
8. Bake about 35 – 40 minutes or until a toothpick comes out clean
9. While the cake is baking, combine the heavy cream, condensed milk and evaporated milk in a large mixing cup

10. Once cake is cool, poke holes all over the cake the more the better so the milk mixture is soaked up
11. Pour the leche all over the cake trying to get every part.
12. In a separate bowl beat the whipping cream, cocoa powder and sugar until stiff peaks
13. Spread all over the top of the cake and refrigerate for about 3 hours or more

COCONUT RUM CAKE

Serves 8-12

*My inspiration came from one of my favorite restaurants here in Miami, "The River Oyster Bar".
They serve a 5-layer coconut cake and when my husband and I ate that we almost fell over
our chair with hoe delicious it was. As I started thinking about how I was going to make my
version Latin version, I immediately thought about adding rum. Rum and coconut go very well
together as a tropical drink so why not make a dessert out of the two. This is one of the most
delicious cakes I have ever eaten!*

Batter

- 3 sticks of butter and a little extra for the pan (unsalted and at room temperature)
- 2 cups sugar
- 5 large eggs
- 1 ½ teaspoon vanilla extract
- ½ teaspoon coconut rum (I use Malibu rum)
- 3 cups flour and a little extra for the pan
- 1 teaspoon baking powder
- ½ teaspoon baking soda
- ½ teaspoon Kosher salt
- 1 cup milk
- ½ cup sweetened shredded coconut (canned grated coconut in syrup is what I use)

Frosting

- 8 ounces of cream cheese (one entire box at room temperature)
- 2 sticks of butter (unsalted and at room temperature)
- ¾ teaspoon vanilla extract
- ¼ teaspoon coconut rum
- 2 cups confectioners' sugar (powdered sugar)
- ¾ cup sweetened shredded coconut

1. Preheat the oven to 350 degrees F and grease two (9-inch) round cake pans
2. With an electric mixer and the paddle attachment, add the butter and sugar and mix together (medium speed) until fluffy.
3. While the mixer is still running, add the eggs one at a time
4. Add the vanilla and rum and continue to mix well
5. In another bowl, add the flour, baking powder, baking soda and salt. Also have the milk ready to add as well.

6. Slowly mix in the milk with the mixer on low and then add the dry mixture in parts. When the batter is completely incorporate, remove the bowl from the mixer and stir in the coconut.
7. Pour the batter 2 pans so that each pan has about the same amount
8. Place them in the oven and cook for about 40 – 50 minutes. (I always make sure that the cake is cooked by inserting a toothpick in the center and when it comes out clean, you are good to go)
9. Let the cakes cool in the pans while you make the frosting
10. In a large bowl (or the same bowl you just used – washed of course) and the electric mixer, same paddle attachment, add the cream cheese, butter, vanilla and rum and mix on low. Then Continue by adding the confectioners' sugar until everything is smooth.
11. When ready, scrape a table knife around the edge of the cake pans. Place a plate on top of the pan and then flip over until the cake comes out.
12. Position the cakes on top of each other with a layer of the frosting in between (if the tops are peaking too much, you can cut them, so they are flat (the part that you cut off is always a good treat to taste the cake prior)
13. Frost the rest of the cake and then sprinkle the coconut on the top and the side

COCONUT RUM CAKE

DULCE DE LECHE FLAN
Serves 6-8

Flan is a dessert that you should learn to make just because of how easy it is and how delicious. When you go to any Cuban restaurant they will most likely always have this dessert and some will have with different flavors. Since my daughter is a true dulce de leche flan, this is the one I decided to learn to make

- 1 cup white sugar
- 14 ounces of condensed milk
- 1 cup milk
- 2 cups heavy cream

- 5 large eggs
- 1 tablespoon vanilla extract
- 14 ounces dulce de leche

1. Preheat the oven to 350 degrees
2. In a small non-stick sauce pan on medium heat, heat while slightly stirring the sugar until completely dissolved and golden brown
3. Remove from heat and let brown a little more
4. Pour into a 9-inch cake pan and swirl the liquid to cover the entire pan and some of the sides
5. Add the condensed milk, milk, cream, eggs and vanilla to a large bowl and mix with a hand held until completely incorporated
6. Pour the mix over the sugar
7. Slowly drizzle the dulce de leche all over the mixture creating a design
8. Place the cake pan in a larger baking dish and add about ½ an inch of water to the larger pan
9. Place in the oven and cook for about 50 minutes or until the flan sets
10. Remove from the heat and from the larger baking dish and let cool about 15 minutes
11. With a dinner knife cut around the edges to loosen from the pan
12. Place a larger plate on top and flip the flan over
13. Chill in the refrigerator until ready to serve

FLAN DE CACAO

serves 6 – 8

Flan is a dessert that is simple to make and very decadent and it looks like you slaved in the kitchen. I have been reading through the benefits of cacao, so it inspired me to add a little something to a classic dish and spice it up a little.

Caramel
- ⅔ cup of sugar
- 3 tablespoon of water – test if I need this
- Non-stick spray

Custard
- 5 large eggs
- 1 (14oz) can Condensed milk
- 1 cup milk (you can use any kind, but I use 2%)
- 1 ½ heavy cream
- 1 tablespoon of pure vanilla extract
- 2 tablespoon of cacao powder
- ⅛ teaspoon of Kosher salt
- Butter to grease the baking dish

1. Preheat the oven to 325 degrees F and grease, with non-stick spray, a 9" round baking dish (you can also use 6 - 8ounce) ramekins
2. In a small non-stick sauce pan on medium high heat, place 1/3 cup of sugar with 3 tablespoons of water
3. Stir well until all the sugar is dissolved then stop stirring and allow the sugar to brown
4. Lower the heat to medium until the sugar has a dark caramel color and remove from heat and pour the caramel into the prepared baking dish
5. In a blender add eggs, condensed milk, milk, cream, vanilla extract, cacao and salt and blend on high.
6. Pour right over the caramel in the baking dish
7. Place the baking dish inside a larger pan (so it fits well) and then add about an inch high of hot water to the larger pan
8. Cook in the oven for about 50 minutes or until set
9. Remove from the larger pan and set aside to cool and then refrigerate for at least 4 hours (preferably overnight)
10. To remove from the pan, cut around the flan, place a large plate on top of the pan and immediately turn over

GUAVA AND CREAM CHEESE ICE CREAM

Makes 6 cups

This is a great story, in 2010 I decided to enter the Paula Deen Philadelphia cream cheese challenge, and this was the first dish I created. Guava and cream cheese on a Cuban cracker was a dessert my dad always had and that was my inspiration, plus the fact that my entire family loves ice cream.

- 8 ounces of cream cheese
- 1 cup of milk
- ¾ cups of sugar (extra fine)
- ⅛ teaspoon of Kosher salt
- ½ cup of heavy cream
- ⅔ cup of guava marmalade (I use Conchita)
- 3 guava shells (small dice) (I use Conchita)
- 12 Cuban crackers (crushed)

1. In a blender, add all the ingredients, except the guava shells and blend together
2. Place the frozen tub on the ice cream maker and turn on
3. While the machine is running, pour the mixture into the ice cream maker and let run for about 30 minutes until ice cream thickens
4. After 20 minutes, add the diced guava shells to the mixture and let mix for the last 10 minutes
5. Pour all the ice cream into a freezer safe container and place in freezer for about an hour
6. Serve and add crushed Cuban crackers on top

GUAVA AND CREAM CHEESE ICE CREAM

KEY LIME PIE ICE CREAM

Serves 4-6

A friend of ours opened a fish market recently and one day while visiting I mentioned that I would love to bring her some of my guava and cream cheese ice cream. She was excited and then asked me if I could also make a key lime pie flavored one. Since I am always up for a challenge, my husband and I ran to the store bought all the ingredients and came up with this recipe

- 2 cups of condensed milk
- 2 cups heavy whipping cream
- 1 cup lime juice

- 1 ready graham cracker crust
- 1 prepared graham cracker crust

1. Mix condensed milk, cream, lime juice and sugar together and cool in the fridge for about 1 hour
2. While the ice cream maker is running, add the mixture and run for about 30 minutes
3. Place in a freezer safe container and freeze over night
4. Crush the graham cracker pie into pieces
5. Serve with the ice cream and sprinkle plenty graham cracker mix on top

POPCORN AND SNO- CAP ICE CREAM

Serves 4-6

Everyone eats popcorn when they go to the movies and many add some chocolate to the mix. I personally love to eat popcorn and sno-caps, in particular. So, one day on a plane on the way back from San Francisco a man told us about a popcorn ice cream he had and proceeded to tell us how the chef made it. Well that got my mind thinking and I came home and decided to put my two flavors together

- 1 ½ cups milk (whole is best but use what you want)
- 3 ½ cups heavy whipping cream
- 1 bag microwave butter popcorn (popped)
- 1 cup white sugar
- 1 box sno-caps

1. In a large sauce pan on medium low heat add the milk, cream and sugar and mix until sugar dissolves
2. Remove from the heat and add the popcorn and let sit for about 15 minutes
3. Strain the liquid into a bowl and throw away the popcorn
4. Chill the liquid in the refrigerator for about an hour
5. With ice cream machine on, add the mixture and let run for about 20 minutes
6. When the mix has thickened, add the sno-caps in batches until completely incorporated about 10 more minutes
7. Place in a freezer safe container and freeze over night

ALWAYS FINISH YOUR MEAL WITH A CAFESITO!

INDEX

Printed in the United States
By Bookmasters